Galileo:
The Man and the Spacecraft

By Carol M. Elliott

Scott Foresman
is an imprint of

Glenview, Illinois • Boston, Massachusetts • Chandler, Arizona •
Upper Saddle River, New Jersey

Photographs

Every effort has been made to secure permission and provide appropriate credit for photographic material. The publisher deeply regrets any omission and pledges to correct errors called to its attention in subsequent editions.

Unless otherwise acknowledged, all photographs are the property of Pearson Education, Inc.

Photo locators denoted as follows: Top (T), Center (C), Bottom (B), Left (L), Right (R), Background (Bkgd)

CVR Roger Ressmeyer/Corbis; **1** JPL/NASA; **4** Time Life Pictures/Mansell/Getty Images; **5** Clive Streeter/Peter Griffiths - modelmaker/©DK Images; **6** ©Gustavo Tomsich/Corbis; **7** Popperfoto/Getty Images; **8** JPL/NASA; **9** © Images.com/Corbis; **10** ©Roger Ressmeyer/Corbis; **11** Roger Ressmeyer/Corbis; **12** Time Life Pictures/NASA/Ames Research Center/Getty Images; **13, 14, 15** JPL/NASA; **16** (Bkgd) JPL/NASA, (Inset) JPL-Caltech /NASA

ISBN 13: 978-0-328-47277-2
ISBN 10:   0-328-47277-8

Copyright © by Pearson Education, Inc., or its affiliates. All rights reserved. Printed in the United States of America. This publication is protected by copyright, and permission should be obtained from the publisher prior to any prohibited reproduction, storage in a retrieval system, or transmission in any form or by any means, electronic, mechanical, photocopying, recording, or likewise. For information regarding permissions, write to Pearson Curriculum Rights & Permissions, One Lake Street, Upper Saddle River, New Jersey 07458.

Pearson® is a trademark, in the U.S. and/or in other countries, of Pearson plc or its affiliates.
Scott Foresman® is a trademark, in the U.S. and/or in other countries, of Pearson Education, Inc., or its affiliates.

3 4 5 6 7 8 9 10 V010 13 12 11 10

TABLE OF CONTENTS

Galileo the Teacher   4
The Telescope Maker   5
Galileo the Astronomer   7
The Earth Mover and Shaker   9
Galileo the Spacecraft   10
Galileo the Probe   12
Galileo the Orbiter   14

Galileo the Teacher

Galileo Galilei was born in 1564 in Italy. At the time, people knew little about the universe. They believed Earth was the center of the universe. They believed the sun, moon, planets, and stars moved around Earth.

Galileo grew up to be a math teacher. He questioned many ideas and tested them to prove whether they were right or wrong.

The Telescope Maker

Galileo liked to study the night sky. At that time, people understood that the other planets moved, but they did not know that these planets had moons. They knew Earth had a moon, of course, but they did not believe Earth moved.

Galileo wasn't so sure. He thought if the other planets move, Earth might move as well.

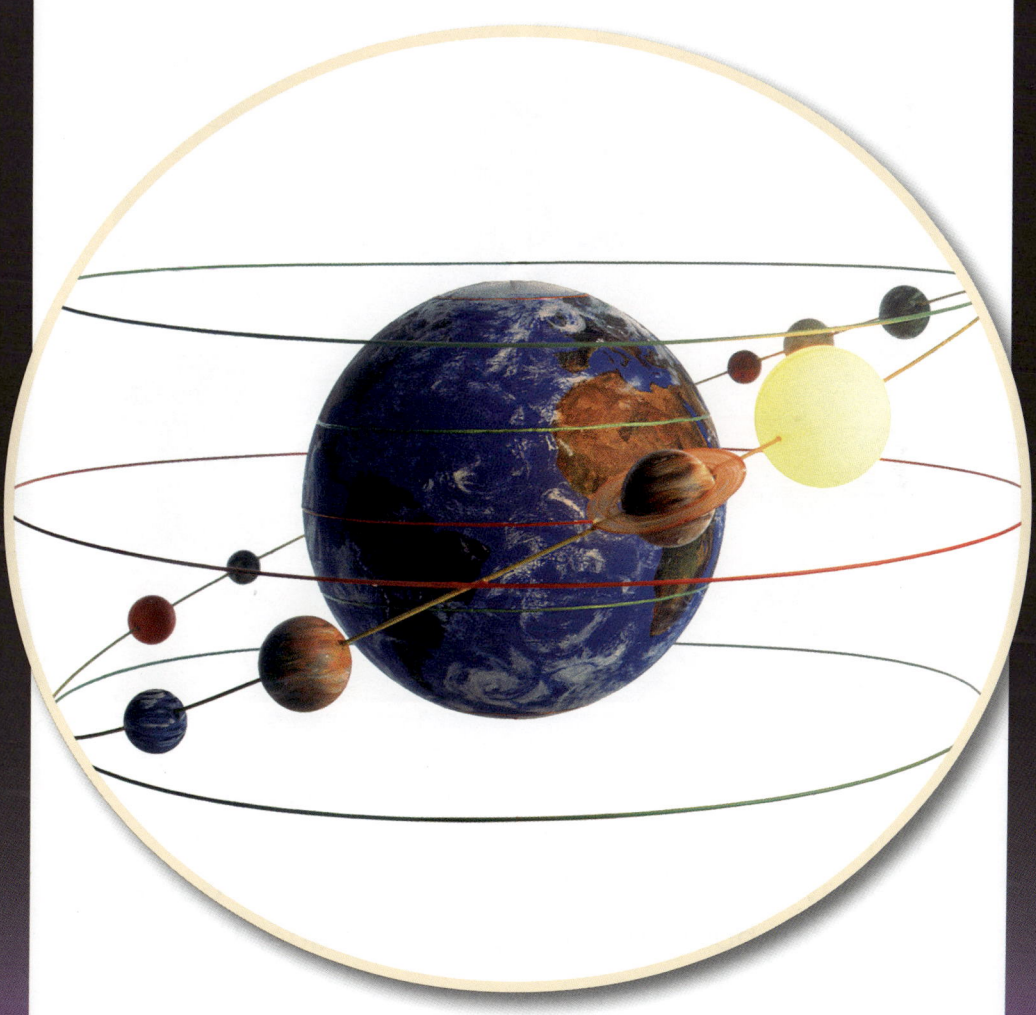

In 1609, Galileo heard about an invention from Holland. It was a telescope, and it made faraway objects appear bigger and closer. Galileo found out how the telescope was made. Then he made his own.

Galileo the Astronomer

Galileo turned his telescope to the planet Jupiter. He saw four tiny spots moving around Jupiter and realized that these spots were moons. Jupiter had moons that no one had seen before!

Here was the proof Galileo needed.

Jupiter's first four moons were named Io, Europa, Ganymede, and Callisto.

The Earth Mover and Shaker

Galileo wrote a book about what he saw with his telescope. He proved that Earth was not the center of the universe, but just another planet. Many people did not like this idea.

Galileo died in 1642. It wasn't until many years later that he was recognized for his important work.

Galileo observed the planets Mercury, Venus, Mars, Jupiter, and Saturn through his telescope on Earth.

Galileo the Spacecraft

More than 300 years after Galileo died, the scientists at NASA, the National Aeronautical Space Administration, made plans to send the first spacecraft to orbit Jupiter.

They named it *Galileo*.

More than 12 years of work went into *Galileo*. It was sent into space in 1989. *Galileo's* journey from Earth to Jupiter took more than six years.

In 1995, *Galileo* arrived at Jupiter. The spacecraft split into two parts—the probe and the orbiter. The probe traveled closer to the planet. The orbiter stayed in Jupiter's orbit and gathered information.

***This is an artist's drawing of** Galileo **and** Jupiter.*

Galileo the Probe

The probe dove toward Jupiter. It was traveling extremely fast—about 100,000 miles per hour. It sent information back to the orbiter. The orbiter then sent the information to Earth.

The probe did not have a camera, but it had seven scientific instruments.

The probe's instruments measured very high winds and temperatures. It showed that Jupiter's weather is very different from Earth's weather. The high temperatures melted the probe's instruments and burned it to ash.

Galileo the Orbiter

The orbiter went around Jupiter and its moons. It carried a camera and 11 other instruments.

It found that the moon Europa has an icy surface. Information suggests that a liquid is under the ice. Perhaps it is water.

Water is necessary for life. Could there be life in the water under Europa's ice?

The orbiter also discovered volcanoes on Io, another of Jupiter's moons. We know now that Io has many volcanoes. The volcanoes are always changing that moon's surface.

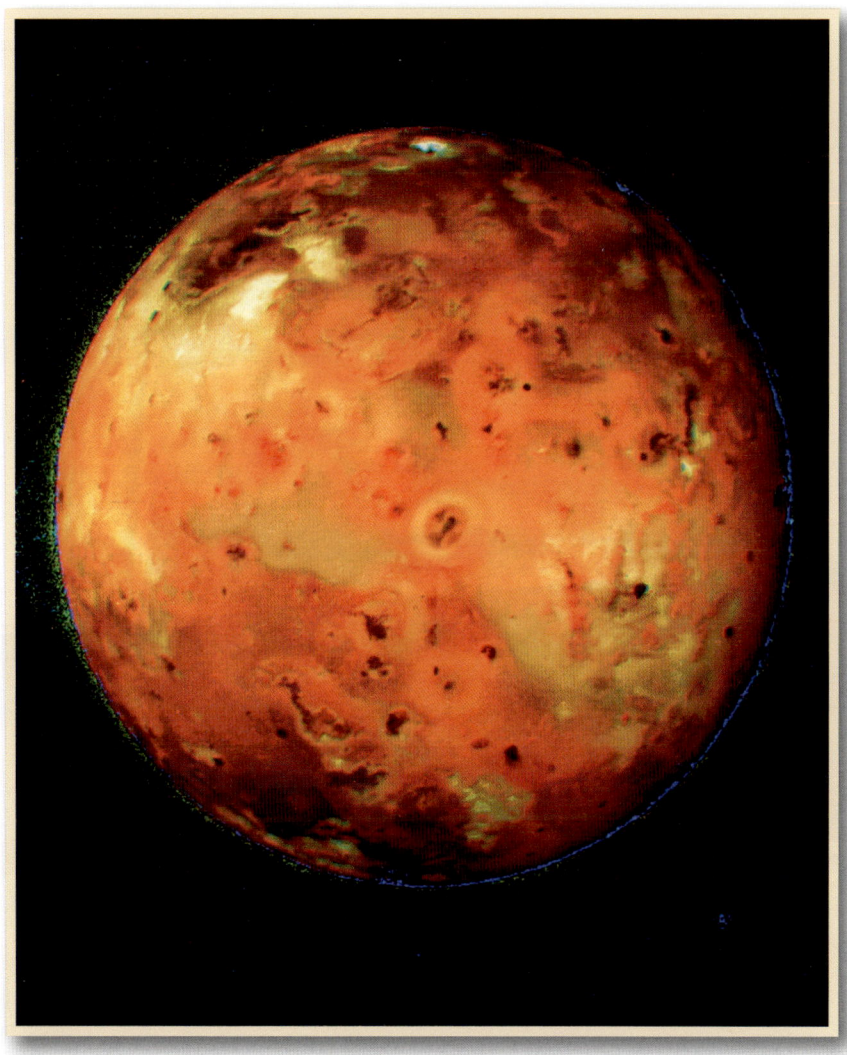

There are more than one hundred volcanoes on the moon Io.

Galileo the orbiter traveled around and around Jupiter for nearly seven years. It fell into Jupiter's atmosphere in 2003 and burned to a crisp. Galileo the man would have been amazed by *Galileo* the spacecraft!

Homes of Tomorrow

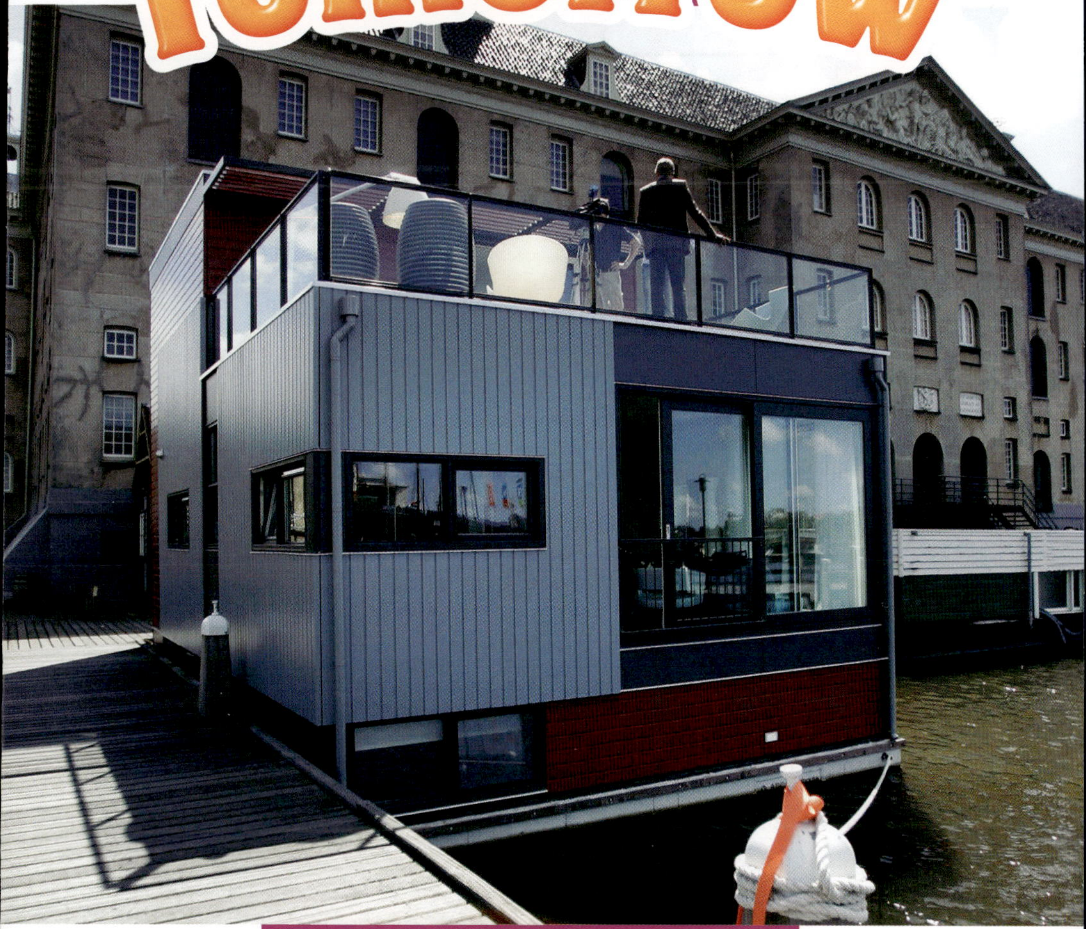

by Mary Lindeen

Scott Foresman
is an imprint of

PEARSON

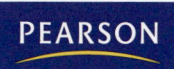

Glenview, Illinois • Boston, Massachusetts • Chandler, Arizona •
Upper Saddle River, New Jersey

Illustrations

7, 9 Jared Osterhold.

Photographs

Every effort has been made to secure permission and provide appropriate credit for photographic material. The publisher deeply regrets any omission and pledges to correct errors called to its attention in subsequent editions.

Unless otherwise acknowledged, all photographs are the property of Pearson Education, Inc.

Photo locators denoted as follows: Top (T), Center (C), Bottom (B), Left (L), Right (R), Background (Bkgd)

Opener: ©Javier Pierini/Taxi/Getty Images; **1** ©Olaf Kraak/AFP/Getty Images; **3** Corbis; **4** Lambert/Hulton Archive/Getty Images; **5** ©Maren Caruso/Taxi/Getty Images; **6** H&LD. Chatz/Jupiter Images; **8** ©Comstock Images/Jupiter Images; **10** ©Javier Pierini/Taxi/Getty Images; **11** VIEW Pictures Ltd/Alamy Images; **12** Kyodo/Landov LLC; **13** ©Martha Cooper/©Peter Arnold, Inc.; **14** (Bkgd) ©Gabriel Bouys/AFP/Getty Images, (Inset) ©Olaf Kraak/AFP/Getty Images.

ISBN 13: 978-0-328-47280-2
ISBN 10:   0-328-47280-8

Copyright © by Pearson Education, Inc., or its affiliates. All rights reserved. Printed in the United States of America. This publication is protected by copyright, and permission should be obtained from the publisher prior to any prohibited reproduction, storage in a retrieval system, or transmission in any form or by any means, electronic, mechanical, photocopying, recording, or likewise. For information regarding permissions, write to Pearson Curriculum Rights & Permissions, One Lake Street, Upper Saddle River, New Jersey 07458.

Pearson® is a trademark, in the U.S. and/or in other countries, of Pearson plc or its affiliates.
Scott Foresman® is a trademark, in the U.S. and/or in other countries, of Pearson Education, Inc., or its affiliates.

3 4 5 6 7 8 9 10 V010 13 12 11 10

Introduction

In 1957, this picture showed someone's idea of the home of the future. Planners thought our homes would look different on the outside.

They also thought our homes would be different inside.

When your grandparents were little, it took a long time to wash dishes by hand. So a machine that could wash and dry dishes all by itself was a very exciting idea.

Now many homes have dishwashers. But people are still wondering how our houses might be different in the future. Years from now, what new **inventions** will we use in our homes every day?

Smart Homes

We might be living in "smart homes." These homes could tell us when to wake up or remind us to turn off the oven. They could even turn the lights on whenever someone walks into a room.

Every room in a smart home would have a computer with a screen built into the wall. On the screen in the kitchen, you could look up recipes for dinner or find out when the pizza delivery person was coming to your door!

Smart homes could be especially helpful for older people. The house could tell homeowners when to take their medicine. Or it could call a neighbor or the **paramedics** instantly if there was trouble.

Moveable Walls and Moveable Robots

As the world gets more crowded, people may have to live in smaller homes. Homes in the future might have walls that move. That way, you could change the size of a room so that you could use it for different purposes.

Many people believe that we'll have robots in our homes in the future. The robots will probably be small, and they'll do jobs such as cleaning the bathroom or closing the blinds.

Materials for Homes

The outsides of our homes might look different too.

Today most homes are built of wood, brick, and glass. But people are trying out new building **materials** for homes.

These **dome-shaped** houses in Japan are made of a type of plastic foam. Dome-shaped houses hold up well in storms. It also takes less money to heat and cool them.

Other people are building homes made of **recycled** materials. Do you think that one day we might all live in houses made of old tires or recycled plastic?

These houses can float. People can build them anywhere that flooding is a problem. When the water rises, so does your home!

Homes such as this one are made from dirt and water, so they're cheap to build. They are safe in an earthquake as well. Some scientists believe these houses could be used for living on the moon.

Many of these changes are hard to imagine, but they may not be that far away. What kind of home do you think you will live in when you are an adult?

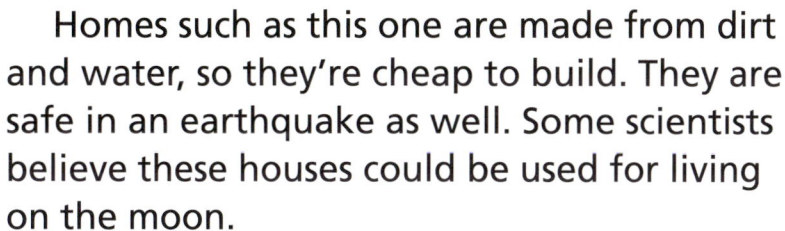

Glossary

dome-shaped *n.* an object in a large, half-round shape, as the top of the capital building is in Washington, D.C.

invention *n.* something new that someone makes or thinks of that didn't exist before

materials *n.* what a thing is made from or used for, such as wood, glass, or steel

paramedic *n.* a person who gives medical help at the scene of an emergency

recycled *v.* when something that was used for one purpose is used again for another purpose